Overcome Public Speaking Nerves And Boost Your Career Without Psycho Mumbo Jumbo, Therapy or Hypnosis!

Why read this book?

Is this you? You are good at your job. You have friends. You are not a social misfit. But, you are literally crippled by public speaking nerves. Small audiences, large audiences, even one important person in a small room - any of these situations can induce a crushing panic attack where the walls close in, and you would rather be swallowed up and die than be where you are. The very thought of public speaking fills you with an immediate stomach churning fear. You are at your wits end. This issue is spoiling you life, dominating your thoughts, ruining your relationships – stressing you out. In others ways you are a normal successful person. You are fed up with hypnosis, counselling etc, as they have zero to limited short term effect and you know deep down they are not tackling the root of the problem. Bottom line, you don't trust these techniques when it comes to the crunch – a public audience, because even after these sessions, you still feel the inner dark sinking feeling even when the remote thought of public speaking is mentioned.

If that description fits, then you need to read this book.

I've been through this. I used to feel that way. Actually, I was worse. **But not now**. I relish the opportunities to publicly speak to audiences that I used to avoid.

If you think your problems are bad, you will know after reading this book that you are not alone and even the most confident appearing people share similar experiences. Actors, politicians, musicians, and your boss – we are all human. What this book tells you is that there is a way of *eliminating* this problem and removing a huge obstacle from your life. It happened for me, and it can for you too. The solution is simple and does not require meditation, breathing techniques or tree hugging. It does not require you to painfully throw yourself into uncomfortable situations, or to see a therapist.

This book is plain speaking, and there are some attempts at humour. I am not a psychologist or therapist. I am not a doctor. I am not a professional author, and I have never written a book before. I have no medical qualifications or experience. I am someone who has suffered horribly from public speaking nerves and literally seen my life and those of others, particularly career wise, **transformed beyond recognition** through the simple solution I have found. This is my honest assessment of what worked for me and could work for you too.

The recommendations in this book may be shocking to some people, particularly counsellors / emotional therapists, hypnotherapists etc as my assertion of this condition is that it cannot be cured or even managed acceptably by the usual techniques they employ. I am not claiming in this text that their methods are useless, or ineffective, but I know they did not work for me and have had limited benefit to others. I have no doubt this text will be jumped on and blogged negatively in many professional pro-therapy forums, but the truth is that my solution **has** worked for me and for many others. Sorry, but this is undeniable fact and many other people have found the same.

To your annoyance, I will stress again and again – <u>I AM NOT A DOCTOR</u>! I am not qualified to recommend drugs and am not recommending or prescribing drugs. All I can do is to share my experiences with you, and if you decide to follow a similar path you should <u>CONSULT A DOCTOR</u> first.

This is a short book. It is intentionally brief (and therefore inexpensive), because the problems discussed are not complicated. I could rattle on for hours about this topic, as many writers do, but the chances are you've already read many books on confidence, self belief, hypnosis, breathing techniques etc, all of which I've found to be overly long and indulgent to their PhD / academic authors, but of little practical use to the normal person who just wants to improve their life without changing who they are or conducting strange rituals before they speak to an audience.

We are who we are. No book can change that. If you are reading this, then the chances are that you are already a smart, intelligent and ambitious person, but being held back by something which is actually more of a physical condition rather than an emotional fault that can be "unlearnt". Through sharing my experience, I hope you will see that the most stubborn of these problems has a solution, and that there is light at the end of the tunnel for you, despite how bad things might seem now.

Let me start by telling you something about me. You might ask why you need to know about me and my background. I think it's important to understand me a little in order to realise I am not that different from you, but also where my fears came from, how bad things got, and how much things have changed for me.

I came from humble beginnings, born into a working class family. None of my relatives had a university degree or had pursued a career. My parents ran their own business, and worked long hours, without much time to spend on my educational needs or emotional support. They did what they needed to do to for us to survive, but I was mostly left to my own devices.

My school years were pretty average. I was smart, but massively underachieving as I became bored very easily. I knew I was reasonably intelligent, but preferred to be the class clown and dodge any hard work rather than knuckle down. I made friends easily and had several enjoyable hobbies. Life was good, apart from one thing that reared its head occasionally – talking in front of class.

Even in the 70's (but more commonly now), we would from time to time be asked to speak about a project, holiday experience - show and tell kind of stuff, but to the whole class of about thirty kids. In any other situation, I was mega confident. I was always happy to do the stupid dare in the park. I would always stand up to the bullies. I was never scared - except for this. I still don't know where it came from, but I guess my ego was so very worried about me failing in front of the class, looking stupid in front of friends, girls, teachers, that I would begin to sweat, feel sick and shake when it looked like I might have to step up.

Annoyingly, some of the weakest, less confident kids seemed to be able to talk confidently in front of class without any care. I envied this. Why couldn't I do that? What was wrong with me? Was I over thinking it? It didn't matter how I analysed it, or which way I looked at it, or how much I told myself it was stupid – I was shit scared, literally to the point of needing the toilet, and would avoid these situations at all cost.

I somehow muddled through school, getting B level grades, and made it to a mediocre University to study technology. Within weeks, it dawned on me that this was regularly going to require me to speak out loud and sometimes make big presentations. For four years, I went through the same painful ritual leading up to a presentation. It started with being told we needed to present something. This immediately started ringing panic bells, that would randomly hit me at all times of the day, and make me sweat *weeks* before the event. As the days to the presentation slowly counted down, the last few days were intolerable: Poor sleeping, continual diarrhoea, stress – all 24 by 7, until the final hours came. Those last hours would result in my head pounding, my body being tired, sickness. I was a defeated person even before I got into the auditorium.

When I actually came to do the presentation, I was shaky, sometimes visibly, and could hardly remember who I was or what I was talking about for the first few moments. Somehow I eventually overcame most of the nerves and delivered an okay presentation. If I got a question or interruption, I could regroup a bit and the initial nerves would back off enough to gain composure. I was lucky in that most of my audiences were keen to quickly ask questions and this allowed me to settle to the point I could control the fear. That was until my final year….

It was my final presentation, a pivotal moment for my four years of study, and one that like all preceding presentations had filled my life with the same fear that someone on death row feels (or at least that's how it felt to me). After seemingly hours of sweaty waiting for my turn, my number was called. I remember feeling actually unable to walk properly, in a daze, confused. I felt extremely unwell. What happened next I can only ask other people to recount. I started my presentation with a semi confident introduction, then started to slur. I then remember a weird metallic taste in my mouth and then a warm fuzzy, buzzy feeling in my head.

In front of two hundred people, I came crashing down like a demolished building, narrowly avoiding killing myself by striking my temple on a very heavy wooden chemistry bench, only a few centimetres from my head.

I was woken by smelling salts. A nurse had been called. People were quietly being led out of the auditorium. She was saying I had "fitted". I knew I hadn't fitted, as I didn't have epilepsy or anything like that, but I did know two things.

One, I had fainted. Two, I had messed myself.

That moment, took my fear of presentations to another level. From that point on, I knew that I could actually faint in front of people, in important situations. It was a huge blow to my confidence, and something I could not hide from myself or talk myself around. It had happened.

Years passed, and I deliberately took career steps which avoided presentations. I knew I was stifling my potential, but I was not prepared to push myself towards a more managerial career which I was very capable of, given that those roles invariably required a lot of public speaking in meetings. However, over time, the inevitable happened.

I was good at my job. *Too good*. Management noticed and I was repeatedly promoted. Over time, it became impossible to avoid having to speak to audiences. Sometimes small, sometimes very large.

The same pattern ensued. Weeks of my life before the event were ruined. I was married now. My wife noticed I would become someone else, even a month before the speech. I would be preoccupied, in another world – a world of pain and anguish. I would talk to her about quitting my job. I even thought about having accidents to hospitalise myself and miss the event. I was messed up. I needed help.

Eventually, I saw a hypnotherapist. I always doubted these types of things, but I was at the point I would try anything. Now, I am not going to say hypnotherapy doesn't work. For some people, it may be the mental crutch they need. But for me, I didn't find it at all helpful. True, it did temporarily boost my confidence and allow me to get into a state of relaxation, which in itself was a relief from the tension I was experiencing, but did it really do the job of stopping the nerves, the fear – no.

I sought other solutions over the years. I took presentation classes. I read books on confidence. I tried breathing techniques. I tried alternative healing. I tried a different hypnotist. But my fear was not going to give in that easily, and the treatments I had tried were not even denting the feelings I had about public speaking. Most of the time I somehow go through the pain of the days and weeks before, and managed to deliver a nervy but half decent speech, until my biggest ever screw up – something that would change my life forever.

I'd been promoted beyond my wildest dreams. Not for my nervy presentations, but for the impact my daily work was having on the business. I was making the firm a lot of money, improving the business, winning the game for them – and they knew it. Even if you are not the perfect manager, you still get promoted and paid more if you deliver the goods, and I was on fire. However, my new title and standing in the firm meant I needed to rub shoulders occasionally with some very senior management, and on one fateful day, I was asked to join a group of key decision makers in a strategy meeting.

The meeting was going well. I was always someone who was able to make ad-hoc comments that were meaningful and added value. I didn't fear group debate or Q&A, it was the solo presentations that made my blood curdle. After a mornings discussion, I was feeling confident, relaxed, one of the "in crowd". I felt I'd arrived and could easily keep pace with these people. I was wrong. Late into the afternoon, I was hit by a curveball. Suddenly the topic swung around to my particular area of expertise and the whole room became focussed on that topic – and quickly focussed on me.

I was given ten minutes to prepare myself to lead the room of twenty or so senior / board level managers through my own thoughts on the problems they were discussing. I didn't have time to worry, I just needed to make some notes and hopefully it would be interactive enough for me to keep my head above water.

The minutes passed in a second. I was up. The room suddenly became more silent and menacing. You could hear the clock ticking and people readied themselves with pens and paper to hear my wisdom unfold. Faces which had looked friendly before, started to transform into serious, concerned expressions. I started to panic. As I began to speak, I could feel my heart pounding, and beads of sweat immediately gathered on my brow. My throat started to dry up and my head was beginning to ring with the familiar sound you hear when you are about to pass out. The walls started to close in, and my vision was blurring. I could hear myself talking, but I knew I was starting to be incoherent. I was in trouble.

Like an awful repeat of the University experience, the next

thing I knew I was in the hands of a medic. This time, an ambulance man. I'd passed out in the chair I was sitting in. Apparently, I slurred my speech, then just leant back and stopped talking. Some people thought I'd died. The room was now empty except for the head of human resources, who had decided to stay with me and hold my hand in support. This was embarrassing beyond belief – I'd fainted in front of the most influential people in the firm. I would be the laughing stock of the office. My career was over.

The only bonus was that my bowels were intact. It's apparently very common for people to wet themselves or evacuate their bowels when fainting. Passing out at work is one thing, but crapping on the boardroom floor – that's unforgivable.

Despite protests, the ambulance took me to the nearest hospital for tests. Company policy. I knew they wouldn't find anything. Weeks followed where I had to have more tests for heart problems, brain disorders etc. Each time I knew they would draw a blank, as I'd just passed out through pure stress. I wasn't actually ill. I finally concocted a story that I had low blood sugar. People at work seemed to buy it, but I knew it had stained my chances of being promoted any further. I felt like a joke, a fraud.

Something had to give. I couldn't go on like this. I hated my job, not because of the work, but these continual situations I had to face – and now, I had the added problem of the fainting incident. People would be waiting for it to happen again. The pressure was at boiling point. I was close to a breakdown.

But I didn't break down. Something amazing happened. I had an epiphany……

"Oh dear", you are now thinking. "This guy is a bible basher and he's going to say he found God, and God saved him from making presentations". Well, you can breathe a sigh of relief. I am a devout atheist, and it wasn't God who saved me, it was science. Medical science.

Now, it's time for me to say once again, and not for the last time, I am not a physiologist, or therapist, but most importantly, I am not a doctor. Nothing I will tell you in this book should be taken as medical advice. I can only tell you what worked for me and what I have observed. If you choose to try the same solution as I did, **you need to consult a doctor first.**

What occurred to me, after having these bad experiences was that I am not mentally or emotionally unstable, nor stupid. I am not timid, socially inept, or lacking intelligence. Basically, it was not my fault that despite my best intentions, this was happening to me. I finally realised that it must be a condition, a physical condition, a medical problem.

So I started to look into what was actually happening to my body during those situations. Could it be that I reacted differently to other people when under stress? Perhaps I had more sensitive "triggers" and needed something to rebalance me, make me more normal?

What I discovered is that whilst we live in a modern world, lacking threats from predatory animals and other enemies, our bodies are still programmed to deal with those situations, and will react independently of our conscious brain to defend us against them in the best way it knows how. We all have an unconscious part to our brain. Our unconscious brain is an amazing thing. Whilst you sleep, something has to tell your heart to beat. When you are hot, something tells you to sweat. When you are in a dangerous situation, our unconscious brain takes charge, and there is really nothing you can do about how it decides to react or what it wants to do!

We are all equipped with something called a "Fight or Flight" mechanism. In simple terms, what this means is that when you encounter a dangerous situation, your unconscious brain prepares you for one of two options – either "Fight" and defend yourself, or "Flight" - run like hell! Whilst the outcome of these two choices can be different, they have one thing in common. Both choices require your body to be prepared for physical exertion. In both cases, blood is immediately pumped hard to your main muscle groups, particularly arms and legs, and this causes momentary low blood pressure in other parts of the body. This can result in some dizziness and a sensation of panic.

Now, for most people, the act of speaking to an audience would not trigger a full blown Flight or Fight response, or if it did, it would be mild and a normal balance would return to the body after a few seconds. What I have discovered is that my own reaction is abnormally severe once it is triggered, and spirals out of control, fed initially by the act of seeing the audience and the anticipation of speaking to a seemingly hostile crowd (actually, crowds are seldom hostile, it's just that the fear inside us projects this onto our overly negative minds), and then turbo charged by the real feeling of panic and loss of control, which in turn sets off increased

Fight or Flight responses in the body, until – BOOM! It's all over, you are out of control and the nerves have won. It's a descending spiral of first anticipating fear, then actually feeling fear, and finally being more fearful because of the physical effects of fear.

In a nutshell, I realised that my body's response to this type of stress is overly sensitive and needs rebalancing. Exactly in the same way some people take thyroxin for thyroid disorders or steroids for asthma, I needed drugs to soften my response to how my body interprets those situations. This explained why all the therapies I had tried had not tackled the problem. It's like going to a hypnotherapist for help with diabetes - it might relieve some of the peripheral symptoms, but it's not going to totally solve the core issue. Even if some of the bad experience can be partially "unlearned" by having more positive experiences at speaking classes like Toast Masters, debating societies or other clubs, and the nerves can be slightly reduced, some people like myself will never cure the underlying problem, as it is one of **physiology, not psychology**.

Having made this realisation and explored the theory, I looked at the options, and came across a startling truth:

People have been using drugs for decades to control anxiety, stress and nerves related to performance

At first, I was shocked, but the more I researched it, the more I found out that there *is* a hidden underground army of people who have realised that they cannot control their body response themselves and need drugs to help them. The list of people I discovered included actors, concert pianists, violin players, guitarists, politicians, teachers, academics, CEO's, even doctors – the list went on. The more I talked to people about it, the more I found other people were doing it or knew people who were. It was sort of an untold but accepted and widespread practice. Everyone seemed to be at it.

So, what is this miracle drug, and how does it work? Well, the drugs in question are called Beta Blockers and here is how they work….

We have to go into a bit more detail and use medical terms (in my capacity as a fully unqualified doctor), so bear with me. Remember I was talking about the unconscious part of the brain? The actual term for the part of the body that deals with stress responses on behalf of the brain is called the Sympathetic Nervous System. The SNS is responsible for administering adrenaline to the body when the unconscious brain thinks you have a problem. For those that don't know what adrenaline is, it is a hormone released when the Fight or Flight response is triggered, and it prepares the body for battle. When adrenaline is released into the blood, tiny cells called Beta Receptors, which are found on the heart, arteries, muscles and airways, bind with adrenaline and send a message to their part of the body to respond. This creates more blood flow in those parts, and leads to the loss of blood in other places. The overall effect is a heightened state of physical awareness: faster heart rate, pumped arms and legs, even keener eyesight. A good state to be in for a physical confrontation, but less than ideal for delivering an articulate speech.

Even when you are not in full Fight or Flight mode, smaller amounts of adrenaline are released by the SNS when you think about stressful things, like a presentation. In people with sensitivity to adrenaline, this can cause anxiety, palpitations, headaches and tremors. Also, because blood is pumped away from places the body doesn't think it needs in battle, like the digestive system, you get stomach upsets because food cannot be properly digested whilst the body is prioritising its resources in other places. I used to experience all these symptoms **_weeks_** before a presentation, as adrenaline slowly leaked into my system as I worried about the event. And the worse I felt, the more I worried about how I felt and how I would perform. A vicious cycle of doom.

So, back to the plot – what do Beta Blockers do?

Beta Blockers numb the sensitivity of the Beta Receptors and lessen the effect of adrenaline on them!

Now, I cannot pinpoint whether I have an over excitable SNS, Beta Receptors, or produce too much adrenaline. It doesn't really matter. What I can tell you for certain, is that taking low doses of Beta Blockers before a presentation creates an AMAZING transformation!!!

Now, you are thinking, "Ok, but I don't want to be pumped with mind altering drugs, as I might feel ok, but I will be high, or talking at one thousand words a minute. People might notice that I am acting weirdly.", or thoughts along those lines.

Relax. Here's what it feels like (and once again, <u>do not take these</u>

<u>without consulting a doctor or physician</u>).

Nothing.

That's right. Nothing.

No rush. No high. No feeling of euphoria. No twitching.

Only one thing……….

A deep, warming and relaxing sense of calm.

And because you are calm, you are confident. Not over confident or complacent, just quietly confident because you don't feel stressed out, and your mind is clear of worry.

The first time I gave a presentation after taking Beta Blockers, I couldn't believe what was happening to me. I couldn't stop smiling afterwards when I realised what I had done. I was able to stand in front of three hundred people, and talk in a professional, relaxed, even inspiring way about my topic. My mind was only filled with one thing – what I wanted to get across the audience. There was no panic, no interfering thoughts about the audience – just clarity, focus, calm! Those little pills were preventing the evil adrenaline from getting to my body and distracting my pitch. And because my body was not in panic, I was able to concentrate on giving the best presentation of my life.

When you are free from panic, your mind is free to think clearly, to consider questions carefully and thoughtfully, to add ad-hoc anecdotes without forgetting things or mucking up the story. You are free to be who you want to be, and to communicate in a senior, professional way.

BB's are not like valium or speed. They do not alter the mind state at all. All they do is to allow the mind to work as it should, un-hindered by the interference of stress and the panic that causes.

Beta Blockers are also definitely not addictive.

What happened after that was astonishing. Once I started to regularly use BB's for any situation that would previously induce a panic, my career took a new direction. I was now not only seen as a good operator, a deliverer of results, but now I was viewed as a master communicator, a strategist, a *leader of people*! My confidence began to swell, and over the next few years, so did my wallet. My career went up so fast, that in the last five years I have got to the point I could easily retire. I have surpassed the careers of my friends and previous peers. I have found new happiness in my work. My home life has improved remarkably, no longer blighted by the torment of the next presentation. Most importantly, I no longer fear those situations at all, and even without Beta Blockers, **I have had so many positive experiences doing presentations that my unconscious brain no longer over reacts to the mention of a public speaking event**. I honestly couldn't care less about having to give another presentation, and it never crosses my mind that I might fail.

Even more positively, over the years, I have told this story to friends and family who suffer these problems. In every case, these people have thanked me over and over again for the transformations they have seen in their careers and personal lives once they started to take BB's for these problems.

So, am I cured?

No.

"What?" you say. Did I just waste my money?

No, you didn't, but you will not be completely cured.

Going back to my point about the condition I have – an over excitable SNS, too much adrenaline, or whatever it is. This will always be how I am constructed. There are no operations, treatments or solutions that can change how I work and how my brain operates. I can now give **fantastic** presentations, which I actually **enjoy** and look forward to. I no longer feel that gnaw of anxiety when I know a big event is coming up. But, don't be suckered into thinking you can give up taking Beta Blockers when you do a presentation. You can't. I've made that mistake, and the harsh reality of how your body operates can quickly come flooding back and you will experience the same old crushing panic you always felt. That's why I always keep a pill in my wallet, in case of impromptu requests to speak. And if I don't have that pill, or enough time to digest it (personally speaking, I need approximately ninety minutes), then I **refuse** to present. That's right, refuse. Nothing can make me go through that hell again, and I have enough confidence now to say to anyone, even the CEO – "Sorry, I need some time to prepare", or in extreme circumstances "Sorry, not feeling good, give me an hour". I **never, ever compromise** on this because I never ever want to screw up a presentation again.

So, are Beta Blockers safe? Sorry, I can't answer that for you, only your doctor can. What I can say is that they were invented in 1962 and have been used by millions of people since in the treatment of a wide range of disorders. Their use as a drug in the treatment of anxiety, particularly what is now termed "Performance Anxiety", has become widely accepted, although controversial within some circles. In particular, some musicians view those performers who take them to lessen stage nerves as "un-pure", even cheating, claiming it takes away the "soul" of the music. In my view, that's just sour grapes from people who also experience stage fright but don't want other people to find an easy solution to something they've battled with for years. Most famously, some athletes such as pistol shooters, archers and others who need a steady hand have used them, although they are now a banned substance given the unfair advantage this obviously gives.

Like all drugs, Beta Blockers have some side effects, and there are some people who have existing conditions or are taking other drugs that should definitely not take them. Again, I am not a doctor, and you should consult a doctor before trying them.

I am actually asthmatic, and BB's should typically not be given to those people with respiratory problems, but my own doctor was more pragmatic and said "Look, you need these, so try a very, very low dose in the safety of your home, and see what happens". BB's give me a little upset stomach which goes after an hour, but that is it. No other issues.

So, that's it my friend. This is my story and it ended well for me. I won't ask you to take Beta Blockers or recommend them to you. I can only tell you my experience and let you make up your own mind with your own doctor. If you've tried other therapies and found them to fail or leave you uncertain, lacking confidence, then this might be the solution for you. Although some people might say that they don't want to be dependent on drugs for help, I've accepted it – I need that help. I have a physical condition, and I couldn't care less about taking a pill if it prevents those awful experiences and helps boost my career.

Good luck, and I wish you a happy and fulfilled life, free of stress and panic about public speaking – after what you've been through, you deserve it.

Printed in Poland
by Amazon Fulfillment
Poland Sp. z o.o., Wrocław